WHERE BEAUTIFUL INKS

The Briny Sea of Poetry

WRITTEN BY:
BRANDY LANE

EDITED BY
VAUGHN ROSTE

CO-EDITED BY
REENA DOSS

FORT WAYNE, INDIANA

© 2023 The Briny Sea of Poetry
Written by: Brandy Lane

Editor: Vaughn Roste
Co-Editor Reena Doss

All rights reserved.
Printed in the United States of America.

No part of this book may be used, stored in a system retrieval system, or transmitted, in any form or any means—by electronic, mechanical, photocopying, recording, or reproduced in any manner whatsoever—without written permission from the author, except in the case of brief quotations embodied in critical articles and reviews.

Published in the United States of America by
Where Beautiful Inks LLC

Fort Wayne, Indiana

ISBN: 978-1-7363268-3-1

Library of Congress Control Number: 2023908562

All pictures throughout this book are available through Canva and Canva Pro.

Dedication

For those left waiting
for the one they love.

A Heartfelt Thank You

Not only am I blessed with a brilliant editor, but I also have a creative team of fellow writers and a beautiful co-editor that assisted me in honing and crafting this gorgeous book. I am honored to give thanks to the following people for their valuable time and influential contributions to the editing process:

Editor: Vaughn Roste

Co-editor: Reena Doss

Proof readers and audible listeners:
Linda Trott Dickman
Chris D. Lane
Stevie Flood
Sharon Andrews
Martin Byrne
Michael J. Dennis
Julie Ann Keleher
Karen Slaughter Steiner

Author's Note

Few of us are lucky enough to find a couple of amazing humans that make the world effervescent—unique souls that turn even the dirt on the ground into something lovely. Perhaps it is their essence, encouraging us to create, making our existence an even more beautiful experience. I have found that magic within my closest friendships.

My dearest companions are not close in proximity, as they are thousands of miles from me. Yet they are constantly in my heart. I communicate with them almost daily. We have laughed together, cried together, loved—and lost together. We have watched each other go through extreme joy and exasperating loss.

These friends keep me humble—yet are there to tell me how strong I am. I don't believe them, but I am still standing, so I suppose that is evidence enough. They are the ones I wish to spend the ins and outs of my days with, no matter our location on the planet. I fervently pray to see them soon and to hold them tightly when that day comes. I suppose this book is more for them than for me. I have already gained the most wonderful part of it all—our beautiful friendships.

A Letter to My Muse

First, you taught me to use my voice to sing with all my heart and soul. Then, you helped reveal my inner voice to set my words on paper, freeing my spirit to be heard. Now, you are teaching me how to weave my words in patterns of poetic artistry.

A mermaid I shall be if it means I can always sing for you—a shiny bauble, something to entertain. All I ever wish for you is that you be content in all that you do. If I may bring you even an ounce of joy, then all of the moments spent in these oceans of emotions are worth it.

Always,

Brandy

Foreward
Written by Stevie Flood

Brandy Leigh Lane is a passionate and talented poet who deeply loves the art of writing. She possesses a soul that seems to be eternally entwined with her muse, and her poetic expressions reflect the intensity of her emotions. Her writing journey began as a way to channel her feelings and thoughts into words, but it quickly evolved into something far more profound.

Brandy is known for her gentle and introspective nature. She is often lost in her world of thoughts, constantly seeking inspiration from the world around her. Her keen observance of the subtle nuances of life allows her to find beauty in the ordinary, and she can effortlessly transform the mundane into something extraordinary through her poetry.

For Brandy, writing is not merely a hobby or a means of self-expression, but an all-consuming passion. It is her way of unraveling the complexities of her inner self and connecting with the essence of the universe. Her poems often explore themes of love, longing, loss, and the human experience, resonating deeply with readers who appreciate raw and heartfelt emotions.

Brandy's muse is an enigmatic force, sometimes elusive and mysterious, yet always captivating. It might be a person, a place, a memory, or even an abstract concept that ignites the spark of creativity within her. When her muse calls, she feels an overwhelming urge to put pen to paper, allowing the words to flow organically and effortlessly.

Brandy's writing process is deeply personal and ritualistic. She often retreats to quiet places, seeking solitude to immerse herself fully in her thoughts. Her trusty notebook and favorite pen are her constant companions, and she finds solace in the act of writing by hand, feeling the ink flow onto the pages as if it were an extension of her soul.

Readers of Brandy's poetry are moved by the profound emotions and vulnerability conveyed in her words. Many find comfort in her verses, as they resonate with their own experiences and emotions. Brandy's writing has a way of making people feel understood and validated, forming a deep connection between her and her audience.

While Brandy Leigh Lane might be a fictional character, she embodies the essence of passionate poets who love to explore the depths of their emotions through their craft. Her dedication to her muse and the art of writing serves as an inspiration to both aspiring poets and avid readers alike, leaving a lasting impact on anyone who encounters her heartfelt verses.

Table of Contents

THE BRINY SEA OF POETRY

TIDAL	3
HURRICANE SOULS	4
CONCH SONG	6
FASCINATE	8
SWIMMING HOLE	10
LOFTY	12
WHAT IF?	14
CAN I?	16
DEPTH	18
SIREN SONG	19
DON'T LEAVE ME	20
SOMEDAY	21
CONFINED	22
SEA OF LOVE	24
PAPER CASTLES	26
INDIGO	28
MY MIND'S DESIRE	29
PLUNGE	30
LIKE THE OTTERS	32
WHAT LOVE'S ALL ABOUT	33
FLOAT	34
SALT	36
I'LL TURN YOU INTO POETRY	38

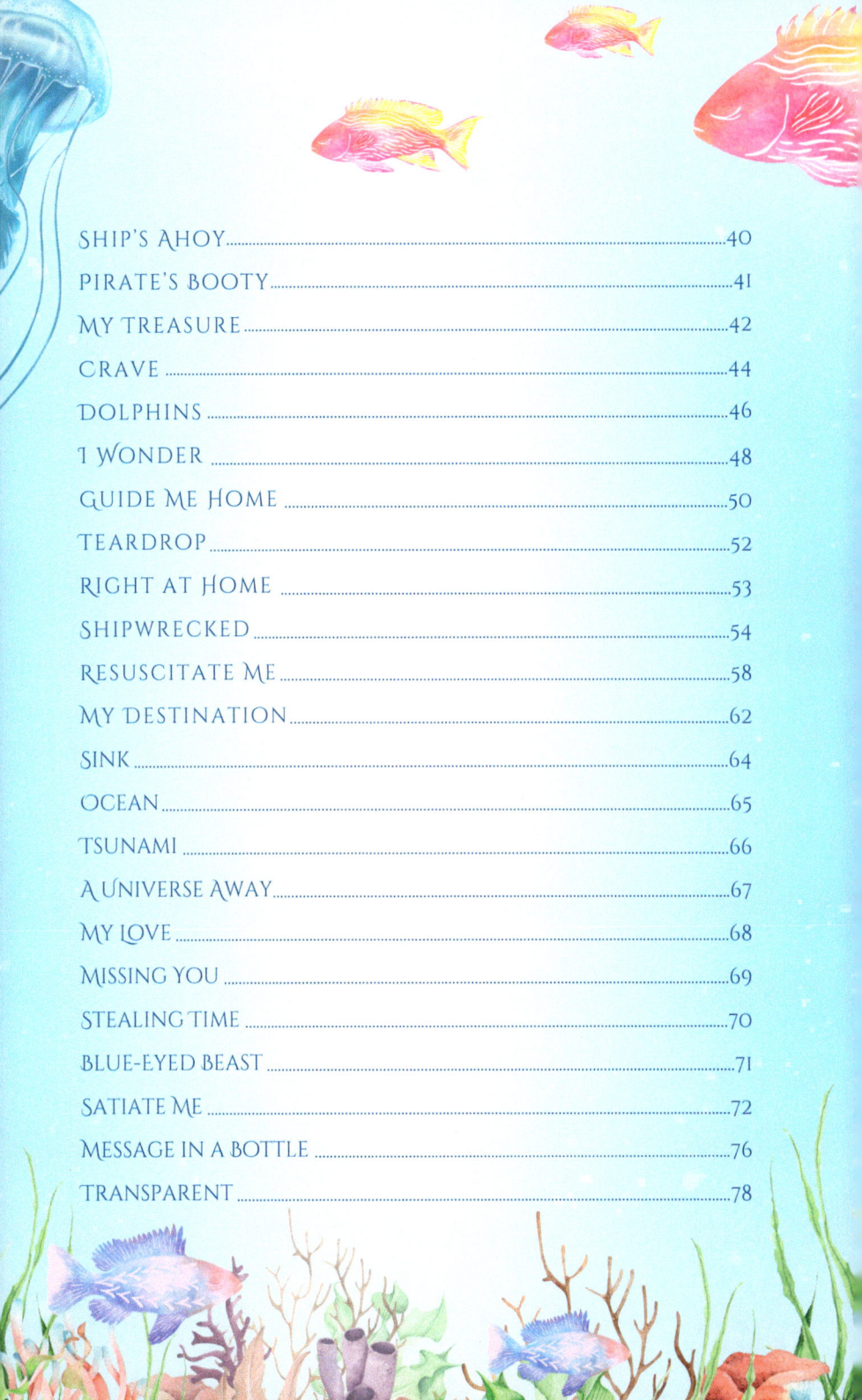

Ship's Ahoy	40
Pirate's Booty	41
My Treasure	42
Crave	44
Dolphins	46
I Wonder	48
Guide Me Home	50
Teardrop	52
Right at Home	53
Shipwrecked	54
Resuscitate Me	58
My Destination	62
Sink	64
Ocean	65
Tsunami	66
A Universe Away	67
My Love	68
Missing You	69
Stealing Time	70
Blue-Eyed Beast	71
Satiate Me	72
Message in a Bottle	76
Transparent	78

On My Mind	80
Walking on Water	82
Floodwaters	84
Puddle	86
Steal Away	87

The Briny Sea of Poetry

POEMS IN OCEANIC METAPHORS

THE BRINY SEA OF POETRY

Tidal

I know how the tide feels,
being pulled by the moon
away from its shore.
You are always steady and welcoming,
and so happy to spend time with me
under that pale, watchful orb.
When he goes, I must follow
in hopeful anticipation of the next time
I may dance upon your shores.

I will leave your tidal pools
full of colorful treasures
as often as I can.
But nothing compares with
permeating your beaches,
saturating your sand,
and the intertwining magic that I feel
as I wash over you in waves.

My salty tears remind me there is hope.
As I find a speck of sand
in the corner of my eye—
it tells me where I have been.
I long for you with all of my depth,
so as to kiss your cheek
as the swells tease so playfully.

BRANDY LANE

Hurricane Souls

You breezed into the room
on a hot day in late summer;
rolling in like a tropical breeze,
steamy and thick.

My heart's depths were churned
as my cold demeanor took notice,
as if awakening from chilly
hibernation.

Our eyes met, and I was lost.

As yin and yang swirl
into chaos and peace,
our spirits began a sultry tango.

You swept me up into your depression,
dark and heavy were your clouds—
my mind ached for landfall.

Lost in thought for quite some time,
never touching earth,
circling above—a dizzying pace.

We became one entity; twirling,
spinning destruction all around us,
but together we were calm in the eye.

THE BRINY SEA OF POETRY

Stillness, quiet, no fear—
for we could see
a universe in there.

We needed each other
to calm
our hurricane souls.

BRANDY LANE

Conch Song

The depths to which I am falling
are unfathomable.
I mean, I knew the oceans were deep,
but this one is a chasm.
Unmeasured.
Otherworldly.

I am bathed in waves of emotion,
each washing over me in rhythms
that guide my heart,
wrapping me in liquid joy,
and engulfing every inch of my body.

Triton himself cannot calm
these seas inside of me,
for they are more magical and powerful
than the sea god's conch song.

He has gone back to the depths
on his cerulean steed
in submission to this love.

THE BRINY SEA OF POETRY

It was inevitable,
that all the years of
salty tears that I've cried,
would turn into this briny sea.

I have grown used to swimming,
and escaping the monsters that chase me... and I
discovered you.

Wrap me in your tentacles.
I will bring you shiny baubles
just to be in your company for a while.
I do not need to fear or escape you,
for you are home to me.

The din of the world
does not dampen the cries of my heart;
it is calling for you always,
like a whale song in the deep.

Longing,
searching,
wanting... you.

BRANDY LANE

Fascinate

I see you,
your graciousness
through pain.

Your joy is great
because of the tears
you have overcome.

You are so deep,
and wonderfully full.

I could spend
a lifetime
diving into you,
getting to know
every single part,
and not get bored.

You fascinate me!

If I were an octopus,
you would be my dazzling garden.

THE BRINY SEA OF POETRY

You enthrall me!

If I were a scientist, I would study everything there is to discover within you.

You entice me!

Every time you are near through music or mere banter, you draw me in.

You make me want to be the best person I know how to be.

BRANDY LANE

Swimming Hole

I could fill a deep pool on a
gorgeous day,
and you would not swim in it.

You might glance at it
and smile,
and even *think* about dipping a toe—
but you are never getting in.

I sometimes wonder...
if I were to break the surface tension,
would I just dive right in?

The thought of cool water
lapping against my body on a hot day;
enveloping me, embracing
every surface of my skin,
holding my breath,
as all my senses are heightened
equally between
beauty and fear—

THE BRINY SEA OF POETRY

I burst upward,
gasping for air,
but willing to dive in
over and over again;
just to feel that closeness
wrapped in my every pore.

But alas, I refrain,
as it is not any fun
to swim alone
and I have been taught that
diving is not safe
and being dry seems to be
the way to go.

Oh, but would it not be fabulous,
just for one afternoon
to lie on the grass
and dry off like sea lions
basking in the sun?

BRANDY LANE

Lofty

The cool air rushes
through my open window,
past my ear, and over my shoulder;
all of nature, the brightest shades of green
from abundant rains.

I am driving, not far in distance,
but my mind wanders
into the loveliness of what lies beyond.
My tethered soul longs to explore,
but finds comfort at home as well.

With a lofty mix
of tumbling clouds
that threaten more rain
and a dash of sunshine,
the sky gives hope for a beautiful day,
with its windy currents
lapping at my skin
as choppy waters would
before a storm.

THE BRINY SEA OF POETRY

The days in theory—
all with the same
seconds, minutes, and hours—
mutate in the realms
of my mind,
distorted into long,
taffy-like simulation
or short and swift,
dependent on
who and what surrounds me
in my moments.

With you,
it seemingly comes back to order...
not too quick, not too long,
never a chore, always welcome,
always refreshing.

Your company
is like a splash in the ocean
on a hot summer's day.

BRANDY LANE

What If?

Now what if I could leave this sea
to fly along with you?
If I could sprout new wings and fly,
yes, that is what I'd do.

Perhaps instead, you'd plunge below,
into the depths with me,
and swim around—but you might drown
in this, my briny sea.

A bird may love a fish, indeed,
but oh, where would they live?
I s'pose they'd die while trying to share
the love they've got to give.

As much as I would love them to,
new wings can't just appear.
And drowning, well, that just won't do,
I'd rather have you here.

So, I shall sing submersed below—
my siren songs to you;
as you fly high, up in the sky
above my ocean blue.

THE BRINY SEA OF POETRY

BRANDY LANE

Can I?

Can I love you indef'nitely?
Forever's too cliché.
Forever's just not long enough,
it's too short by a day.

I'll cheer you till the end of time
until the sand's last grain.
As wrinkles form along your cheek,
each time you smile again?

To be enraptured by your soul
whilst looking in your eyes;
the light that grabbed me at first glance,
and took me by surprise?

To think about your sweet embrace
as I drift off to sleep;
whenever I feel lonely and
my sadness, much too deep?

Can I recall your vibrant laugh,
the way it fills the room?
It booms with such ultimate joy,
to chase away all gloom.

Can I keep you inside my heart
until it beats no more?
'Cause you're the one I care about:
the one it's beating for.

Depth

The love inside me is calmer now,
and in these still waters,
I can feel the depth
even more than I could before.

My darling,
whales be swimming deep within...
they meander in my stomach
every time I think of you.

The octopus has wrapped
his tentacles firmly 'round my heart—
squeezing tightly as it beats,
changing colors with my mood,
as cuttlefish do.

There is warmth and chill,
nothing, and all,
encompassing
my being.

You are still the pirate
that has captured my heart
but I'll admit,
you never had to steal it.
It was freely given.

Turns out,
you were never a pirate at all—
just a beautiful adventurer
that happened to cross these waters.
Perhaps, it was I who answered
your siren song.

THE BRINY SEA OF POETRY

Siren Song

Mermaid blood sings through my veins
in melodies for you.
This desire can't be quenched—
I thirst for you, it's true.

Our hearts pulse in harmony,
whilst in your arms I lay.
But, my home is not with thee;
therefore, I cannot stay.

Cast me back into the sea!
I'll dive below the depths;
these emotions will not fade,
they'll conquer even, death.

I prefer this ache inside
to what I felt before.
Carrying this burden 'round
is now a happy chore.

You have been my destiny
for all recorded time.
All I know is I am yours
and in my heart, you're mine.

Don't Leave Me

Have you ever stood at the ocean
with the waves crashing at your feet,
then watched how
the water that was left behind,
runs back toward the sea,
almost as if to say—

"Don't leave me,
I am part of you."

That is how I feel
every time we say goodbye,
as though you have saturated
every particle of me,
leaving parts of you within me,
and they want nothing more
than to get back to you.

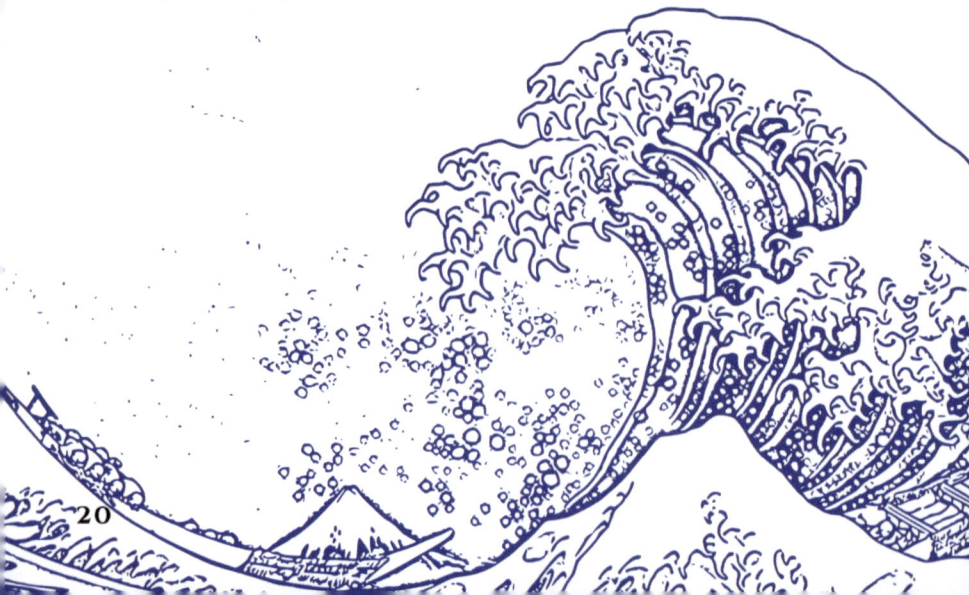

Someday

Someday, I'll get my life in place,
and all of my past sins, erase.
I'll do the things I've wanted to,
all that I have put off to do.

I'll travel to the other lands,
to oceans and their distant sands.
Perhaps amongst the sharks I'll dive,
a moment to feel more alive.

I'll rule the sea with peace and light,
no one will ever fuss or fight.
We'll work and live and laugh and play,
If I can make it to someday.

Confined

How many ways
can I think of
to tell you how I feel?
Words don't come close.
Art, music, poetry...

A kiss?

Why does this intensity live within me?
Wanting to get to you.

Like a fish in a bowl...

I can see you, but you're out there
and I'm in here, swimming in circles.
I cannot be with you,
and you would
drown with me.

THE BRINY SEA OF POETRY

So I spend my days dreaming.
I imagine what life could be like...
Again, it's my soul
that is trapped.

It is the fish, and my flesh is the bowl.

My soul constantly feels confined within this body,
as though it remembers being free before.

The day I met you, it grew restless—
like there was so much more to learn,
to experience,
to feel.

Alas, to escape

would mean the death of me.

BRANDY LANE

Sea of Love

From out of nowhere, waves of love
smack me from out the blue!
I'm floating in this water—filled
with naught but thoughts of you.

These grandiose ideas swim
along with whims and notions,
just as the whales of giant size
meander through the oceans.

These verbal trickles might seem small,
to some, they're rather tiny,
but they together form a sea
that's vast, yet very briny.

Your eyes are azure, and I see
a depth so very blue,
and that the love you hold for me,
reflects my love for you.

BRANDY LANE

Paper Castles

Love trickles in...
like a sprinkle of rain
splashes the cheek,
grazing it gently
like the softest kiss.

The downpour is overwhelming
as love floods in,
bringing joy in abundance.
In my mind,
you placed the stars
in the sky.

What started as a surprise,
became constant.
Trickles turned to splashes,
downpours to floods,
floods formed into oceans.

The evaporative fancies have flown,
and I'm left with depth.
A bond understood,
a beautiful embrace in friendship—
each time we're together.

We don't just form
kingdoms in our minds,
we are building paper castles
with our imaginations.

THE BRINY SEA OF POETRY

Our words, though separate,
are hand in hand
in the pages of books.
I never thought of a book
as being a chorus,
but perhaps, I should;
souls combined in harmony,
as each combines to tell a story.

Even though it's quiet,
our voices are still heard.
There's a comfort in the silence,
as we are nestled in the pages—
souls bared on paper
for the world to see.

Caught between the sheets,
trapped for all time—
until we are freed to roam
in the imaginations of those
whose fingers turn the pages.

Like the genie in a bottle,
we beg to be freed,
to be allowed to play together,
in every mind that reads the pages
to which we've so carefully
inscribed our words.

I will always find you...
as we live on immortally
within the minds of others.

BRANDY LANE

Indigo

Ah, Indigo! So deep and blue,
the color that I feel for you:
your eyes' depth, much like the sea,
I drown in their eternity.

Your soul's desires are all in view,
your aura glows with vibrant hue—
yet the light surrounding you,
is bright, yet dark, indigo blue.

THE BRINY SEA OF POETRY

My Mind's Desire

Dearest lover of words,
my mind's desire...
You are the steady palm
on the island of my dreams,
the stars that guide my raft
on the ocean.

You keep my thoughts company
when my mind is adrift;
my balloon aloft—
when my head is in the clouds.

Your touch is gentle,
like the swaying fronds on the
ocean breeze.

You are my companion
in the silence of the night,
and my comfort
in the chaos of the day.

Whenever I am alone,
I think of you,
and you are the only company
I desire.

Plunge

The weekend will be here very shortly—
it feels months away in my mind.

Every hour that I cannot get
to see, talk, or write to you—it's ridiculous!

We all need our space, I just happen to want you in mine.
I could dreamily stare into your dancing eyes—forever.

You are such a comfort to me, and I want nothing more
than to wrap myself in your company.

You are so chivalrous, being strong and restrained—
not letting me overstep, keeping me at bay.

I want to cliff-dive, but you are holding me safe,
and reminding me that still-waters run deeper.

I am flabbergasted by the way you make me feel—
if I could reciprocate even a portion.

My heart is so full, after being empty for so long.
I never even realized how depleted I was.

I wonder how I make you feel,
if you are stirring around inside
as I am—
if you can see
an entirely different world
in my eyes,
as I do
when I plunge into yours.

BRANDY LANE

Like the Otters

Whenever one of us
starts to drift,
whenever we are wandering...

I will do my part
to keep you near,
to keep you company,
to be your friend.

I will be an anchor
when the waves get choppy
and help pull in the sails
when storms approach.

I want you to know
that I'm here for you.
You don't ever have
to be alone.

THE BRINY SEA OF POETRY

What Love's all About

From highest heights to depths of sea,
I'll show you what you mean to me—
in song or in reality
or maybe through more poetry.

For all the love I have for you
is vast and wide like oceans blue.
If nothing else, my heart is true
and these emotions, far from few.

So here it is, my heart poured out:
(although I want to scream and shout)
to tell the world to have no doubt,
for this is what love's all about.

BRANDY LANE

Float

Glossy waters,
reflecting
the beauty
around you—
gentle sounds
as the oars
splash and drip.

Cool and clear
and so inviting
as salty sweat sits
on your brow—
to take a dip.

Diving under,
enveloping
every pore,
taking your breath
but for a moment.

Floating freely
on your back,
clouds in the sky
look upon you...

THE BRINY SEA OF POETRY

You are free.

BRANDY LANE

Salt

There is a portal in my mind,
where I may go whene're I want.
It is the most intriguing place,
I find you there often enough.

Today, it took me to the sea;
the grains of sand fell 'tween my toes.
We walked along the shore all day.
How many miles? No one knows.

Spray from the waves, ever so slight,
was misted on my cheeks and lips—
so when I licked, I tasted salt—
a sav'ry way to end the day.

The foamy sea came to my toes,
alluring me in tempting ways—
a wayward captain lost at sea,
the siren sang her song to me.

I listened to her brazen call
and went knee-deep into the bay;
took pleasure in the haunting sound
and very nearly drowned that day.

THE BRINY SEA OF POETRY

BRANDY LANE

I'll Turn You into Poetry

I'll turn you into poetry
and make everyone see you
as a masterpiece.
I'll take each memory I have
and with the stroke of a pen,
fill books with nothing
but your essence.

Everyone who reads my words
will know you by your soul.
Magically, the drying ink
glitters on the paper,
as it adheres to the fibers;
the way your soul
entwines with mine.

I hold my breath,
not wanting this feeling to wane
and just float here, for a while,
wishing it were endless.
Oh, these waves
like seasons, come and go.
I'll wait eagerly
for when the surf gets high.

I want to crash into your soul
with the force of a tsunami.

These seismic tremors
in my depths have been gathering
in cataclysmic abundance for so long,
just waiting to burst forth.
I'm left with these little earthquakes,
holding it all inside,
except for my mind,
and now your mind,
as you are reading.

If I cannot grab your soul, your heart;
perhaps your mind will allow
me to dance with yours.
My thoughts intertwine with yours
into a beautiful waltz.
I stare into your eyes,
as you guide me along
the marble floors.
Spinning, yet the dizziness I feel
is more from the butterflies
that reside in my stomach.

You hold me like the breeze
holds the delicate wildflowers;
my butterflies feel at home
in your presence.
They become still, and I can
once again exhale.

I am finally at home, here with you.

BRANDY LANE

Ship's Ahoy

The scallywags are sleepin',
a mighty lazy crew!
But fine for me,
I'll have some tea,
or coffee I will brew.

My ship is still a floatin',
been docked for many days,
but prepped for sail;
the wind's at tail—
to soon sweep me away.

I'll voyage to your island,
bind you to make you mine.
I'll make you treats,
massage your feet—
it shall be so divine!

I'll give you everything!
I'll honor you as King!
All my doubloons,
my heart in ruins—
my name, to hear you sing!

THE BRINY SEA OF POETRY

Pirate's Booty

"Why, ships ahoy, there matey!"
he said, whilst ousting the sail.
His shirt then blew off in the wind;
a gust, not quite a gale.

His feathered hat he captured,
right as it tilted down.
With that, his mouth curved into shape—
a simper, not a frown.

He glanced up and he winked,
his eyes a gentle blue—
the tint of sky in light of day,
not of the midnight hue.

He turned to walk away.
But, oh! Those leather pants!
I must admit that booty-full view
had me quite entranced!

Quite flushed, I fanned myself,
and if I may be bold,
I think I've found the treasure, oh!
That booty is pure gold!

BRANDY LANE

My Treasure

We'll sail around the world
with the sails unfurled,
boarding ships for a dance,
in your tight leather pants—
a heart-breaker to all guys and girls!

You'll keep them all entranced
stealing hearts and minds at a glance.
I'll collect all the treasure,
and giggle with pleasure
'cause they never had a chance!

One day I'll realize,
there's a longing in your eyes.
I'll give up the gold
as they say, "turkey, cold"
and I'll drop my clever disguise.

I'll realize you ARE my treasure,
my love beyond all measure.
I will send you away,
while praying you'll stay,
on your own, at your very leisure.

I'll drop you off at the shore,
loving you forevermore...
I'll say my good-byes,
sailing t'ward horizon'd skies,
aching right down to my core.

BRANDY LANE

Crave

I crave, I want, I need you...
There's nothing to quench this thirst.
I could try each thing on Earth,
I'll always want you first.

Excursions to the kitchen,
whilst hungry late at night—
wine, nor cheese, nor sug'ry things
can satisfy this plight.

I drank up all the vino,
and here I am again,
desiring to be with you
but there's no way I can.

An ocean lies betwixt us,
and many miles of land—
keeping me from seeing you,
and from your gentle hand.

THE BRINY SEA OF POETRY

How can I overcome this?
I'm in starvation mode!
There must be some great mystery
that I can decode.

Send me a magic portal,
that I can step inside...
All I need to be with you
are dreams to be my guide!

I lay my head on pillows
and finally find that door...
I get to hold you in my arms,
till daylight comes once more.

BRANDY LANE

Dolphins

The constant flow of love
I have for you
never slows.

It is never in drought;
just ever-abundant
and bursting to get to you.

These thoughts jotted down
are mere minnows
on the surface of this vast ocean.

Unfathomable depths
where love reaches
even the darkest places.

I feel the dolphins
jumping in my stomach
whene'er I think of you!

THE BRINY SEA OF POETRY

BRANDY LANE

I Wonder

I wonder if the mermaids
make wishes on the starfish—
as we do on the stars
that are hung up in the sky.

Or if they watch the stingrays
while gliding through the ocean,
as we gaze at the kites
that are dancing way up high.

I ponder if they journey
to visit all the wonders;
a trip down to the reef
or the great shipwrecks of old.

Or if they look for treasures
the octopus had buried,
like abalone, pearls,
or big, wooden trunks of gold

I wonder if the storm clouds
take pride in when they're crying
while they watch as their tears
turn to oceans down below.

I wonder if the water
understands from whence it came—
inside a giant tree
or from mountaintops of snow.

I wonder if the oceans
within which whales swim
are all the fallen tears
I once had inside of me.

I wonder if all the tears
wept since the dawn of mankind
in pain, joy, or sorrow,
have become the salty sea.

THE BRINY SEA OF POETRY

Guide Me Home

The one I cannot have,
he, whom I cannot hold...
His gentle hand, as I caress—
entwining fingers fold.

He's there when I'm alone,
so deep within my mind...
I feel him in my heart and soul—
a tether that doth bind.

This feeling never fades,
it only grows with time...
Anticipating times like this—
just makes them more sublime.

Burning inside of me,
it cannot be contained—
no distance, nor no barricade
can keep this love restrained!

I thought that parting ways
might dim this dancing flame—
so bittersweet and passionate,
yet it cannot be tamed!

A beacon from afar,
illuminates the night
as though I'm lost out on the sea,
I follow its bright light.

With you, I know I'm home,
comfort not felt before—
oh, guide me to your harbor now
so I may come ashore.

Teardrop

Watery orbs
streak like snails
down my face,
leaving trails of salt
where the makeup
used to lay.
I watch them drip
onto my lap,
as my dress absorbs
the brine of me.

I feel as though
I am an island,
as you are far away
from me.
I look out
over the vastness
and wonder
if the sea is nothing
but the collected tears
of lost loves.

THE BRINY SEA OF POETRY

Right at Home

I've settled down
upon this ship,
out on this salty sea
and whispered wishes
from my lips
to send to you from me.

The waves,
they rock me back and forth,
just like a metronome—
reminding me that
when you're near
I'm always right at home.

BRANDY LANE

Shipwrecked

My mind is in a flurry,
as if I'm caught in a storm
on the ocean—and cannot see my way home.

I am navigating inch by inch—
going through all the motions,
 but I cannot see you!

The mist and foam,
the undulating waves,
are unrelenting.

Seaspray stings my bleary eyes,
 already wet with tears.

Where is my lighthouse, my beacon?

Where am I going?

I am just spinning here in circles,
seeing the same things go by
over and over again.
It never changes,
never calms.

Oh, Triangle of Bermuda,
let me be!
Allow your magnetism
to release me on my way!

THE BRINY SEA OF POETRY

*But I know
I will reach home someday,
if I can just keep going.*

Alas, exhaustion ensues,
the stormy blues and grays,
and the flecks of white
that color the clouds are upon me,
and I cannot turn away!

I must weather the storm
through to the other side,
but at what cost?

Must I crash against the rocks
in the sea and lose everything?
Why not abandon ship
and dive in now?

If I beseech King Triton to embellish me
with the scales and fins of a mermaid,
I could sing others back home!

Dash these dreams—
these fairy tales,
these colorful reasonings
of my mind that tend to fail!

But... they do make for lovely poetry
that allow my mind to sail away
for moments at a time.

continued

What of my reality,
 as I drift away on stormy seas
without your love to guide me?

What if I cannot take this
battering anymore—
the pelting rains against my face,
the howling winds in my ears?

This nightmare has to end!

I wish a dashing pirate
could come and steal me away
in his white silk ruffled shirt
and rather tight pants...

We'd sing songs all night
and count our doubloons! Casks
of rum be of plenty!
We'd dance the night away...

There I go again,

catching a dream

for smoother sailing—

in my mind.

I must find a moonstone
for this ancient compass to work again,
for the stars are veiled
and my horizon is askew.

There isn't anyone
who can hear me asking for directions
in this vast abyss.

I might as well be deaf!
And dumb!
And blind!

*For I cannot see past this fog
and my wits are not about me.*

No one is around
to hear my screams or cries
and no one can see my words.
So I'll send them in this bottle now,
for someone to see
long after my ordeal is over.

Maybe they will be shared
for me to come across again someday
or maybe they will float aimlessly
in the waters such as I do.

Resuscitate Me

When I say "I love you,"
it is from my core.

Love has so many meanings,
but the last thing I want it to be is a filler.
I don't want it to be a thoughtless chirp
on my way out the door.
I don't want it to be given
in mindless quips.

No, I'd rather say it with the oceans
that I feel within my depths,
when the waves
are knocking me off of my feet,
when seismic tremors rush through my heart,
as I feel every part of the universe
rumble toward my mouth,
as I am gazing upon your soul...

THE BRINY SEA OF POETRY

...I want to be breathless
upon the whispered forces—
pushing it through my lips
as the oceans leak
through my eyes
and breathing the words out—
is <u>the only option.</u>

I want it to be
life or death to my existence—
that if I don't speak,
I will never breathe again
because it would be against
all of life and God
and all of His creations
not to.

continued

I want to be held accountable
for loving.

This cosmic, wonderful,
all-encompassing,
soul-baring–yet-crushing feeling
inside of me.

I'd rather just know you love me...
I don't need to hear the words
if I already know.

So when the day comes
that I am gasping,
breathless on your shores...
the last thing I will need
are your words.

When I am that far gone,
I will need your actions,
pulling me from the abyss,
resuscitating me with your breath
and combining your soul with mine.

Then, and only then
will I know—

*I don't want to be drowned in love,
I want to be saved by it.*

My Destination

I left you upon the shore,
and dove into the sea.
I swam away, tears streaming,
adding to the volume of the salty brine.

In my mind,
I imagine you looking out at the sunset,
wondering if I'll ever return;
wondering if I was real
or just a fleeting dream.

My song has grown faint,
a din in the back of your mind.
In comparison, I still hear fanfare
where're you're concerned.

Know this:

my destination
will always be
whatever shore
you are standing on.

I'll fight the mighty Kraken,
escape through the whale's blowhole,
to find a way to be with you again.

BRANDY LANE

Ocean

Ocean,
full and mysterious—
never knowing what lurks
just below your surface.

I want to dive
into your epitome,
and discover all that is hidden
in the cold shadows;
down to where the light
no longer breaks through.

I want to explore every cave,
every life form, every shell,
every vessel...
of you.

Original artwork by Brandy Lane

THE BRINY SEA OF POETRY

Sink

I wish to burn
into the sinking sunset,
disappear
into the night,
shoot across the sky
like falling stars.

I want to vanish
into the wind,
sink beneath
the ocean waves,
decompose
into the sea's
sandy floor.

My head, aching.
Stomach, turning.
Heart, breaking.
Soul, yearning.

BRANDY LANE

Tsunami

Trying to ignore this feeling
is like trying to deny the ocean's existence
in the midst of a tsunami.

I just can't.

Even with every storm wall,
every barricade I've tried to
put in place.

The feeling consumes me,
breaks me down
piece by piece—
until I'm flooded once again
with love for you.

THE BRINY SEA OF POETRY

A Universe Away

Stuck in your universe,
I cannot break free
from your gravity.

Sometimes smiling,
sometimes hiding
in the shadows.

I go through phases
as you watch me from afar—
basking in the light.

You expect me to stay
day in and day out—
always there, staring at you...

...with your oceans,
your snowy peaks,
your tumbling clouds.

I can never touch you
or hold you,
or call you mine...

And I can't help that I sway
your waters;
ebbing and flowing your tides.

I see you, I feel you,
I'm always with you
but you're still a universe away.

BRANDY LANE

My Love

My love transcends the heights and depths,
the shadowed corners, and the breadths
of anywhere that you might be—
a mountaintop, valley, or sea.

It finds you in the vast abyss
when everything's askew, amiss,
and pulls you back through space and time,
brings back the rhythm and the rhyme.

My lofty thoughts of trees and sky
and of the birds in clouds so high
float, aimlessly in search of you,
amongst the atmosphere of blue.

They soar to altitudes not flown,
a love so rare no one has known—
up where the crystals form, then fall
to kiss the cheeks of one and all.

I pray one lands upon your face
with such a soft and gentle grace,
that you can feel the warmth of me
within that icy filigree.

And as it melts upon your flesh,
your soul will feel renewed, refreshed—
absorbing deep into your skin,
migrating to your heart within...

Missing You

I am missing you
in ways that poetry cannot fill,
where food is bland
and my thirst is never satisfied.
Crowded rooms feel empty,
and no one seems familiar.

I am missing you
like the ocean waves at the beach
as it retreats, then can't stand
being away—so it rushes back
to kiss its sands one last time—
over and over again.

I am missing you
in the solitude of the night;
when the coyotes howl in the distance,
crying for one another.
I feel a kinship in their hollow howls,
awaiting a response.

I miss you most
when I close my eyes.
I can almost feel your touch
and imagine your breathing.
I conjure dreams
just to be close to you again,
for they seem so real,
and there are days
I find it hard to awaken.

I miss you as much
as the polar ice caps
miss their frozen masses
as they calve into the waters,
never to rejoin.
They melt away into a briny sea,
much like my tears,
mourning the distance
between us.

BRANDY LANE

Stealing Time

All this time, you were worried
that you would come crashing
down from the pedestal—
the one you claim I fashioned for you.
But can't you see?
You were never on one
to begin with.
From where my broken body,
barely standing,
still adores your precious heart,
I look across the table
at your kind eyes and adorable smile.

Like glints of the sun
off the peaks of ocean waves,
the love you have for me
still glints through,
though overwhelmed with life
within a sea of chaos.

I still see you.

The glimmer of your soul
is exhausted but still shining.
I feel the same as you,
wanting to give so much more—
but unable to conjure
the strength or the time
as the clock ticks relentlessly
toward its final destination.

THE BRINY SEA OF POETRY

Blue-Eyed Beast

Gorgeous beast
with bright blue eyes,
fly me up
into the skies!

We'll explore
the edge of the sea;
into the caves—
just you and me...

I'll find the wood,
you light the fire—
while sharing tales
of our desires.

Playing games
and drinking wine,
gazing at
God's vast design.

All I need
is your company—
in our little cave
at the edge of the sea.

BRANDY LANE

Satiate Me

*I awaken in the morning
immediately craving
words from you;
missing the feasts
of intimacy we'd share.*

*Wanting so much to see
your twinkling eyes;
your face all aglow
with dimpled passion,
teeth reflecting sparkles of light,
like dolphins breaking
the water's surface.*

THE BRINY SEA OF POETRY

I miss the banter our flesh shared
upon the slightest touch;
how electricity would
ravish my skin in
goose pimples,
at even the suspicion of caress.

It was never the wine
causing the intoxication—
as water harbors the same effect
as long as I am
in your presence.
Perhaps water-into-wine
is a biblical metaphor,
as I have first-hand knowledge of
spiritual tipsiness.

continued

BRANDY LANE

Oh, my soul needs you,
it is barely holding on.
I am not as aware of
my body, my mind,
the hairs on my head,
as I am when you are near.
I miss the way the down on my neck
would stand in titillation
over the breeze of you
when you'd sweep by me,
when you'd breathe.

The way the timbre of your voice
would boom within my chest
as though it were
the bass of a dance floor sub-woofer,
shaking me from the inside.
I miss being immersed
in the sheer awe
of everything you are.

I'm no longer going to be silent.
This silence has made
my world—unbearable
intolerable;
like the bland porridge fed
to each poor bastard
in every black-and-white movie
to depict how awful things were.

I've now tasted
the brown sugar cinnamon,
butter, raisins and I'd rather starve
than go back to gruel.

Like Dorothy on her path
to finding her way home,
I now see in color.

Every time I close my own,
I see your blue eyes
staring into my soul.

I am hungry for a feast;
only you can
satiate me.

THE BRINY SEA OF POETRY

Message in a Bottle

Like a bottle aimlessly at sea
or airmail before this century,
there's no way to track my words.

I'm listless, awaiting a reply,
of any sort, of any kind—
unless "no reply" is your answer,
not even "return to sender"
just unanswered questions.

Love, unrequited.

THE BRINY SEA OF POETRY

Transparent

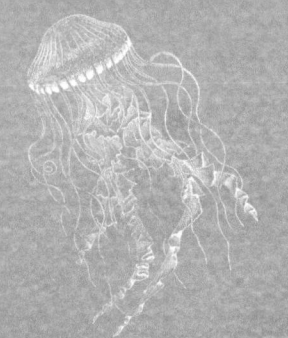

I am floating on the currents, but you can barely see—
for I am near-invisible, out in this great big sea.

You might meander past me with nary a suspicion,
but, I might sting you without care, void of all contrition.

I'm not here to be your friend, I guess that is apparent.
Avoiding me is hard, after all, I AM transparent.

BRANDY LANE

On Your Mind

There are so many things
that I refrain from saying,
as though I'm keeping
my real self at bay.

All I ever want to do
is drown you in my love,
then resuscitate you
back to life;
plunge into you with all I have—
then recede slowly,
leaving nothing but beauty in my wake.

I want to brush your lips
with the ease of the ocean's current, caress you
as you sink to its floor.

Then lift you as the bubbles,
back to where the ocean meets the sky.
I want to be the tension at the surface
as you break through from water to air.

THE BRINY SEA OF POETRY

I long to kiss
your goose-pimpled flesh
as the reflective prismed droplets
glisten on your skin
as you emerge.
I want to greet you as the
brilliant sun,
wrapping you in my warm rays.

Then I want to be the sand
between your toes
as you walk home with me—
on your mind.

BRANDY LANE

Walking on Water

Gazing over emerald grass,
pondering what life has thrown at me, my
mind always meanders
to that ethereal place
where I can spend time
with you.

Love is love,
and I'm not one to fight love,
but what else am I to do
with this abundance of emotion
that washes over me in waves?

Just like the water on the earth...
I need it.
I crave it.
I thirst for it.
I want to bathe in it.

But... if I'm not careful?
I would drown in it.

Oh, I've tried to walk on water,
frozen it to skate upon
in the dead of winter—
as the snowflakes landed on my face
and promptly morphed into tears.

THE BRINY SEA OF POETRY

The screeching sounds of the blades
as I would turn in circles,
just before the toe pick
would slam down
with a loud crack
and the force would launch me
into the air.

That is what you have done for me—
I was flying, instead of drowning.
Alas, what goes up,
must come down.

Turning circles in the air,
the lightness I feel is ephemeral...
I carefully land back on one foot,
balancing...
looking for your hand.

Winters melt into spring
and walking on water
is no longer an option,
much less flying.
I find myself treading water...
hoping to find land.

BRANDY LANE

Floodwaters

And I still write but not as often,
because there are dams in place;
ones that I wish we'd never built...

I can feel the floodwaters rising,
pushing against them,
trying to make them
crumble.

No dam
can still the ebb and flow
of the swirling depths
inside of me!

Oh, how I wish to be free
to flood you with love,
to saturate with abundant waves
and trickle down into the hidden places!

I want to envelop you
within my waters
and carry you off
to cerulean seas.

THE BRINY SEA OF POETRY

Can you not see it in my eyes?
Can you not hear my longing soul?
It constantly cries out for you.

Yes, I remember...
I never have forgotten,
not for a single moment—
that I did this all
because of love.

I always will—
as long as you are in my life.

BRANDY LANE

Puddle

Closing my eyes,
I dip my toes
in the puddle
of memories
I have with you.
Splashing through
the moments
refreshes
my weary soul.

THE BRINY SEA OF POETRY

Steal Away

Steal away with me, beneath the sea,
we will dive to the fathoms below.
We will swim and play the day away,
as we're frolicking hither and fro.

Let's find a cove with a treasure trove
that the pirates have long forgotten,
then lie on the land with its soft sand
on fluffy white towels of cotton.

We'll gaze from the coast, cuddling close
as we watch Sun's meandering rays—
you'll steal a kiss that I'll reminisce
every day for the rest of my days.

Acknowledgments

So grateful for the editors and publishers that have included the following poems in their anthologies and magazines. The poems, many times in their rawest and earliest versions, appeared as follows.

"The Octopus" cover art by Brandy Lane was originally published in Ink Gladiators Press', *The Fall and Rise of Chimera's Autumn Seasonal* (Dec. 2020).

"Conch Song" was originally published in Ink Gladiators Press', *The Fall and Rise of Chimera's Autumn Seasonal* (Dec. 2020).

"Siren Song" was originally published in RDW World's *Unabridged Version December Edition Poetry 365* (Dec. 2020).

"Indigo" was originally published in RDW World's *Unabridged Version November Edition Poetry 365* (Nov 2020).

"Hurricane Souls" was originally published in Red Penguin Book's *The Ocean Waves* (July 2021).

ALSO PUBLISHED IN

Poetry 365 by RDW (both abridged and unabridged editions) for November, December, January, February, March, April, May, and June, and special editions of Creator, Hope, and Self Portrait editions.

Red Penguin Books has published her pieces in 'Tis the Season's, The Flower Shop on the Corner, The Ocean Waves, and Bloom Issue 2 magazine.

Clarendon House Publications published her poems in their Poetica 2 and Poetica 3 anthologies.

Ink Gladiators Press' anthologies of The Rise and Fall of Chimera's and Gray, We Hide our Colors Within.

Indie Blu(e) Publishing just published a mental health piece in Through the Looking Glass: Reflecting on Madness and Chaos Within, and their newest anthology, But You Don't Look Sick: The Real Life Adventures of Fibro Bitches, Lupus Warriors, and Other Superheroes Battling Invisible Illness.

300 South Media Group has published her in As Darkness Falls and features her first flash fiction piece in Sunset Rain.

Train River Poetry has published her in Poetry 7.

Who's Who of Emerging Writers by Sweetycat Press.

Harness Magazine in their November 2022 issue.

Silent Spark Press Amazing Poetry Volume 13, 2023.

About the Author

Brandy Lane

Brandy Lane has lived most of her life in Indiana and Colorado, where she resides with her husband and four children. She published her first book, **Where Beautiful Loves**, in December 2020 under her imprint, **Where Beautiful Inks**. Just after the release of her first book, she discovered anthologies as an option for publishing and has since had poetry pieces included in over three dozen publications. In 2023, she curated and edited, **Winter, A Poetic Anthology** which is a collaboration of 25 poets from all over the world. It spent 5 days at #1 in New Releases in Anthologies on Amazon.

A hopeless romantic, Brandy draws inspiration mainly from nature, but also from human connection. Her poetry is much like her personality, showing vulnerability as well as strength. The muse that she writes to is someone who taught her she is worthy of love, that she is "enough" and yes, "sometimes more than enough." She finds beauty in every situation, which sometimes is her greatest curse.

In her spare time, she loves spending time outdoors in the mountains, taking in the sublime views. She also loves a good board game, and video chatting with her favorite friends all over the world.

Brandy can be found online: on Instagram @wherebeautifullives and Facebook @Where Beautiful Lives

ABOUT THE EDITOR

Vaughn Roste

Canadian by birth, Vaughn Roste currently lives in Chicago, Illinois. He is a published author of books, plays, poems, peer-reviewed articles, book reviews, program notes for CD liners and Carnegie Hall, and a doctoral dissertation. His first book, The Xenophobe's Guide to the Canadians, was published by Oval Books in England. He has two WWII films currently in pre-production, ORADOUR and THE NINE LIVES OF WALKER HARRIS. His 20-min short film FIREFIGHTER was produced by M3 Studios and is available on Youtube, and another script entitled WORST. FILM. EVER. is scheduled to be shot later in 2023 by Milepost42 Studios. His stage play, THE NAME OF THE GAME won the Leo Award for Best Overall Script at the 2021 Da Vinci International Film Festival for Best Overall Script, beating out features and shorts - the first time a play has been awarded this prize. He is represented by Jason Bellitto at Citizen Skull.

ABOUT THE CO-EDITOR

Reena Doss

"I'll find you in the dark because I'm the girl who loves to stay lost amongst the midnight stars caught up with moonbeams in a lantern trying to find my way back home."

Reena Doss considers writing to be her first voice of expression, followed closely by art and creativity. Through the encouraging platform provided by the Instagram community, she reclaimed her lost voices, evolved a few others and discovered new ones along the way. This has redeemed her trust that consistent Hope, Faith and Love in what is true ignites what is impossible to occur. Her adoration for her beloved Weaver, the Celestial Sky, Nature and her fellow Earthians has given her immeasurable courage to endure every season with a resilience born from battles overcome. She also showcases her artistic talents at His Wild, which features her digital paintings and shares her passion for children's literature at The Pickleton Universe by working on kid lit books for the future. Reena is also the Founder of Ink Gladiators Press where she publishes theme based work in anthologies under the names—Our Earthians Community Group and Translations Of Hope, reviews self-published books and recommends self-publishing services at IGP Ship. Overall, her voices are a reflection of her personality, life story and unwavering faith.

Currently, she resides in Bangalore, India but loves traveling to far-off places inside her head and sometimes, in the world that others call real. You can try and catch her on Instagram at reenadossauthor but it may not always be possible as she is generally off on adventures chasing dragons, phoenixes and mermaids down for stories. www.reenadoss.com

OTHER TITLES FROM BRANDY LANE

WHERE BEAUTIFUL LOVES

POETRY AND PROSE BY
BRANDY LANE

OTHER TITLES FROM WHERE BEAUTIFUL INKS

WORKS IN PROGRESS

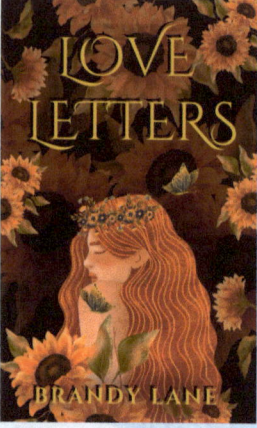